Deborah's

ROAR

Discover your authority; unleash your roar.

Ikisha S. Cross

Deborah's Roar
Discover your authority; unleash your roar.

Copyright © 2024 Ikisha Cross

Unless otherwise noted, Scripture quotations marked (KJV) are taken from THE HOLY BIBLE, KING JAMES VERSION. Public domain.

Scripture quotations marked (CEB) are taken from THE HOLY BIBLE, COMMON ENGLISH BIBLE, Copyright © 2010, 2011 by Christian Resources Development Corporation

Scripture quotations marked (AMP) are taken from THE HOLY BIBLE, AMPLIFIED, Copyright © 1954, 1958, 1962, 1964, 1965, 1987 by The Lockman Foundation

Scripture quotations marked (ESV) are taken from THE HOLY BIBLE, ENGLISH STANDARD VERSION, Copyright © 2001by Crossway, a publishing ministry.

Scripture quotations marked (NLT) are taken from THE HOLY BIBLE, NEW LIVING TRANSLATION, Copyright © 1996, 2004, 2007 by Tyndale House Foundation. Used by permission. All rights reserved.

Published By: Judiyah Publishing Company
Cover Art Design By: Kirklin Cross Jr.
Edited By: Shana Washington – shanaspeakslife.com

ISBN: 978-1-7374135-2-3

Table of Contents

Dedication

This book is dedicated to my beautiful daughters
J'Ohnnye, Aniyah, Daelyn, Kellan, and my fierce,
unstoppable, ROARING Daughters of Truth Church!

Introduction

Before beginning this journey, let's pause to thank our faithful God. I always want to ensure that in these moments He's the focus and thank you is always in order. So, let us unite in inviting our Father, asking for His guidance to lead us through this sacred endeavor.

Let us pray:

Opening Prayer

Father, we bless you, we love you, and God, we thank you for choosing us and honoring you in us. Father, I pray now in the name of Jesus that you be in the midst of us and that your power and your anointing arrest us. Father, speak your word to your people however you decide. Father, I surrender this vessel and ask you to clean me up now, so that your spirit will flow freely. Whatever you have mandated and ordained for this moment will be accomplished because Your spirit has led us into this time. Father, I surrender. Be God! Speak to Your people in the name of Jesus, Amen.

Chapter 1

Deborah the Patriot

I want to give praise and thanks to the Almighty for you being here with me on this incredible adventure delving into the life of Prophetess Deborah. I'm just so thankful. Every day, my husband and I are on a mission to spread and evangelize this good news, bringing as many souls as we can into the Kingdom. I give all honor to God and His spirit, recognizing the phenomenal way it sustains us, leads us, and guides us on this journey. We're going to be in Judges 4. The focus scripture is Judges 4:8-9 where we're going to deal with Prophet Deborah as the patriot.

The Common English Bible says, "⁸Barack replied to her 'if you'll go with me, I'll go; but if not, I won't go.' ⁹Deborah answered, 'I'll go with you. However, the path you're taking won't bring honor to you, because the Lord will hand over Sisera to a woman. Then Deborah got up and went with Barack to Kedesh" (Judges 4:8-9).

I'm going to go ahead and set the stage so you can understand where we're going. So here we are in Judges 4, Israel sinned against the Lord, AGAIN! The third judge died, and God turned them over to the Canaanites. He let them be oppressed for 20 years, at which time Israel decided to cry out to the Lord from their oppression and the torment they put themselves in! Sounds familiar, doesn't it? Look at our world today. God has allowed us to be in a situation where we are being oppressed and tormented because we have turned our faces and our hearts away from God.

So, when a cry emanated from Israel, Go heard them! Deborah minding her own business was caught off guard and moved her from a comfortable state into her call. Often, we find ourselves becoming complacent and settled, until God shakes us awake from our slumber. I recall when the Lord called me; I was content where I was. Suddenly, He disrupted my life and unsettled me, revealing that a cry had come out from the earth for what He put in me. When I think of Prophet Deborah, the term "trailblazer" immediately comes to mind. She epitomizes a patriot, one who staunchly supports their nation and defends it against adversaries and detractors (Oxford Learner's Dictionary). I've come to understand that patriots are born in response to injustice. We often associate patriots with those who go to war because of some injustice. Similarly, Deborah responded when a cry emerged from Israel. God essentially said, "Deborah, I know you're comfortable where you are, but I need YOU!"

Now, let's examine Deborah more closely. First and foremost, Deborah was an uncommon choice. If we examine the scriptures, most, if not all, of the judges, except for the fourth, were men. Deborah was not a man's choice; she didn't fit, she measured up, they never saw her coming! However, God made the choice. He mandated the uncommon choice because of the cry from Israel needed an uncommon response. God needed someone He could trust, someone who would obey, someone man couldn't control.

Secondly, Deborah embraced her identity. She believed in who God said she was. This gave her authority and rank.

Often, we profess belief in God, yearning for rank and authority. We seek it out and pray for it. But do we truly believe in who God says we are, based solely on His word? You see, there's no scriptural account detailing how God called Deborah. She simply appeared on the scene. There was no grand announcement, she simply responded with BELIEF. We must grasp the notion that all we need is a word from the Lord. Deborah didn't seek validation from people. She didn't seek permission. God said, "Be," and she replied, "Yes, Lord." This made her usable. Can God use you?

Thirdly, Deborah was bold and unwavering. Throughout history, it was unheard of for a woman to hold such a position, especially when the Lord called her to lead in battle and defeat the oppressors. Deborah boldly declared, "Bring me Barak, so I may deliver to him the word of the Lord." When she spoke the word of the Lord, she did so with unshakeable courage because she knew God had spoken directly to her. She understood that in God, she possessed everything necessary to fulfill her role. Deborah embraced her identity in God and her significance to Him. Consequently, she confidently summoned the general, stating with authority, "Listen, this is what the Lord has spoken."

If we refer to verse 6, it states, "She sent word to Barak, Abinoam's son from Kedesh in Naphtali, and said to him, 'Hasn't the Lord, the God of Israel, commanded you, 'Go, take with you ten thousand men of Naphtali and Zebulun and lead them up to Mount Tabor? Verse 7 "I will lure Sisera, the commander of Jabin's army, with his chariots and his troops to the Kishon River and give him into your hands.'" She queried Barak, asking if God had indeed given him these instructions. She conveyed a message to the general, which included specific instructions. Then she said, "Listen, here are the instructions, and while you're following them, I'll assist you in overcoming them." Barak understood WHO SHE WAS and WHO SENT HER! He recognized her authority and fearlessness in the face of death.

Finally, Deborah wasn't swayed by the odds. She didn't yield to circumstances; instead, she was motivated by them. If we examine the scriptures, the Canaanite army had nine hundred chariots of iron. Yet, Deborah confidently declared, "God said He will deliver them into your hands." Deborah wasn't concerned about their weaponry, their reputation, or their numbers because God promised to deliver them into Barak's hands. Barak just needed to hear and obey. Barak received the word, but Deborah ensured he understood something. She said, "Listen, the path you're choosing is fine. Just understand this, this victory will NOT come by your hands but by the hands of a WOMAN!"

WOMAN- Listen! Deborah wasn't the popular choice among men, but there was a cry that came out of Israel, and God chose a WOMAN to answer the cry! She didn't fit, she wasn't popular, but she was CHOSEN! We still wonder why we never fit in anywhere, why we were never embraced in these systems. It's because God needed us, and we were mandated and ordained as the unconventional choice. WOMAN, YOU ARE GOD'S response to a cry from the Earth. God entrusted us to be defenders, as the Bible discusses being defenders of the faith. God called us to be defenders and to defend vigorously. That's why we never fit in. That's why it never came together. We spend our lives trying to be accepted in places God never intended for us to be accepted. We were built not to fit in because God called us out of comfort and into authority and dominion. God called us to be defenders and patriots.

In the midst of it all, we must grasp the power of God's word. It doesn't matter if others aren't recognizing the validity of your calling; If they never call you "it", it doesn't mean you're not! Hold onto what God has declared over your life. Align yourself. Agree with God. When the Almighty called your name, it wasn't a conference call! He singled you out and said, "You." So, we must move away from seeking validation from people for what only God can authenticate. When those men and women of God come your way, it's not just a coincidence; it's a confirmation because your spirit should already know!

Since we're not the conventional choice in our own eyes, the problem lies in our response to God. We don't respond because we fear what it will look like. We fear people murmuring or complaining. We're entirely appalled and traumatized by what somebody might say about what the Lord told us to do. I bind that in the name of Jesus, and I release and lose those chains from your ankles. I command you now to walk fearlessly in the very thing God has ordained and sanctioned you to do.

Deborah was unconventional, but she believed in God, and because of her belief, she was fearless to the point where she summoned a general and issued instructions to him. The general was so attuned to what the Lord was saying that he said, "I'll go if you go with me." Based on my knowledge, Barak didn't express doubts or fears about the size of the opposing forces. Instead, Barak simply stated, "Woman, if you go with me, I'm going."

As you continue to grow in your understanding of who you are in God, becoming fearless and fully embracing your calling, the lives you impact, cover, and encounter will witness firsthand what it means to trust God in seemingly insurmountable circumstances. They will have testimony, evidence, and an example of what it looks like to have unwavering faith. They will observe you, the patriot, embodying the role God has called you to with courage. Through your example, they will begin to believe in God and His word, and they too will become fearless. Consequently, the obstacles and odds stacked against them will no longer intimidate them.

The pains you've endured, whether growing up in poverty, in a single-parent home, or experiencing abuse, will cease to hold power over you or your descendants. They will recognize that they have a word from the Lord, and because they witnessed a patriot in action, they will start to believe that the same God you serve is their God too. They will begin to reproduce your faith and fearlessness, ultimately creating a generation that trusts God! Refusing to be defined by their circumstances. They will not be swayed by obstacles because they received a word from the Lord through the mouth of a Patriot.

Thus, you will begin to multiply, as there will be a conviction in your spirit that because God spoke a thing, you can surely accomplish it. As you fervently defend and inspire others to embrace fearlessness, these patriots will become PIONEERS. This calling is not exclusive to certain groups of people; the adversity you've faced is because you were meant to be a pioneer. A pioneer is someone who develops or is the first to use or apply a new method area of knowledge or activity (Oxford Learner's Dictionary).

By obediently responding to God's call and acting as a patriot, you ultimately become a pioneer. God will use you to pave the way, just LIKE Deborah! Causing many more women to step into God's call. Through the uncommon choice of Deborah, a path was forged because she was an unexpected choice, she believed God, was fearless, and refused to be deterred by circumstances, God said, "I will make you a trailblazer."

You may be wondering why you've endured such much. It's because you were the one chosen by God to blaze the trail. You were selected to be the pioneer because God could trust you. He knew that if you understood the identity He had given you, many lives would be saved because you chose to trust His voice. That's why you are the curse breaker. That's why you can look back over your life and see where others didn't make it out, GOD'S HAND WAS ON YOU!

You can reflect on instances where you should have been dead and recognize the reality of it because there were situations where you should not have survived. Yet, God heard the cry and raised you, guiding you out of those dark places and setting you on a path to BLAZE A TRAIL!

What the enemy intended for your destruction; God turned around for your elevation! You are the unexpected, the one they never saw coming. Did those judges, all those men, ever think God would choose a woman? They doubted, they gossiped, but God declared, "You are the one!" About a decade ago, the Lord spoke to me, saying, "Kisha, I called YOU, not who you pretend to be!" We must align ourselves with God's word over our lives. We are called not only to be patriots but to blaze the trail, to be the first, and to do so with strength. It's challenging because we're breaking new ground, but that's the divine calling, my friend.

There is no manual, beloved. You are undergoing on-the-job training because you are the trailblazer, the groundbreaker. You are the one laying the foundation. Tending to the soil in your garden is no easy task; it's a disruption of the ground, a labor of love. It requires sweat and movement. And let me tell you, it's been tough for you because you are the one handpicked by God to write the guidebook. You, my sister, who has experienced it all—former prostitute, recovering from addiction, battling alcoholism—you are the chosen vessel. Don't make excuses or list all the reasons why you think you're not qualified. God has His eye on you; you are the one He's calling.

Sis, let me share this revelation with you—this prophecy is tailor-made for you. Yes, it has been YOU all along, from the very beginning. The adversary is working tirelessly to silence you and keep you feeling low. Why, you ask? Because he knows that if you summon the courage, if you boldly embrace the fact that God has CALLED you, you will shatter the barriers in your life and break the chains for generations past and to come.

Let me make it plain; your mother might be bound until you align yourself with the purpose God has specifically called you to fulfill. Your father's breakthrough might be waiting for you to embrace the calling God has placed on your life. And what if it's your grandmother? Her liberation might hinge on your resounding "YES" to God. Picture this: as you step into your divine assignment, the schemes the enemy has plotted for your children will crumble into oblivion. God's plan for you is a mighty force that annihilates the schemes of the enemy. So, beloved, say yes, and watch the miraculous transformation unfold!

This isn't just about us; it impacts our generations! Align yourself with God, find your voice, and embrace your purpose, you will begin to roar at the enemy and declare, "They weren't brave enough or courageous enough, BUT I AM! I'm not scared. You won't have anything else from my lineage in Jesus' Name." The devil will realize that if you're not afraid of him, he has no power over you.

What made Deborah so powerful was that she understood her authority and her authority in God. Often, we become fearful because we focus on our authority rather than God's authority. However, when we truly understand that heaven backs us, we won't be intimidated or timid about speaking up. That's the roar of Deborah—it's the mechanism through which God has mandated us to lead His people back into His presence, to discover their unique sound from God.

Presently, many sounds are emanating from the Earth, but they are not the sound of God. We must enter a realm where we embrace, capture, and accept God's sound within us. Listen, I'd love to sing like Fantasia. Scratch that; I just want to be able to holler like her. But that's not my sound. The truth is, I used to be too concerned about how my sound was perceived by everyone else, but when I realized that the sound God gave me was the one He wanted to hear from me, it set me free. ROAR PATRIOT... ROAR PIONEER!!!

Closing Prayer

Father, we love and thank you. I pray now in the name of Jesus that your people come into a better understanding of who the patriot and pioneer is in them. Father, for every moment of uncertainty, fear, and anger that causes us to abort our patriotism and the pioneer that you placed inside of us we repent, for every time that we were concerned about what it would look like, who would have something to say about it, we now see how we rejected you and your call because we were afraid. We repent! Father, we decree and declare that the patriot and the pioneer are alive and well in us. Father, we come into alignment with what you've spoken fearlessly because we have received a word from You. Father, we declare that you are enough, and your word is enough. Father, I pray that the person reading this book is strengthened in their spirit man to pursue You in a greater way. God, remind them that being the uncommon choice is Your choice. God causes us to be okay with being chosen. Father, we love you and we appreciate you. Thank you for Deborah the patriot, in Jesus' name Amen.

Chapter 2

Deborah the Judge

In the last chapter, we celebrated the fact that Deborah was an extraordinary pick. She exuded fearlessness, courage, and boldness. Deborah was a trailblazer and a trendsetter, yet she embodied even greater depths. And let me tell you, God was right there with her every step of the way. So, let's dive into, Judges 4:5 where the word says, "She held court under the Palm of Deborah between Ramah and Bethel in the hill country of Ephraim, and the Israelites went up to her to have their disputes decided" (Judges 4:5 NIV).

When we talk about a Judge, we're talking about a public servant appointed by a governing authority to make decisions in the court of law, according to Oxford

Languages. So, let's journey into where our sister Deborah held her court. The Holy Spirit whispered to me, "Kisha, take note of where she was seated." And swiftly, it became clear - between Ramah and Bethel. Ramah means lifted and exalted, while Bethel means the House of God. Prophetess Deborah sat between a high place and the very House of God. Now, in those days, the judges of Israel had their chambers, or thrones to judge. The Book declares something different for our sister Deborah, the fourth judge of Israel. No chambers, no thrones for her. The Word says she was seated under a tree. Oh, what a revelation! Deborah is not confined to the lofty seat but rooted under a tree. The place where God sat Deborah speaks to God's covering. Under the shade of His wisdom, strength, and stability. MIGHTY GOD!

Let's look at the symbolism of the palm tree because honestly, I was confused. Why did God put her under a tree? After reviewing the significance of a palm tree, I discovered that the palm tree is a symbol of victory, triumph, peace, and eternal life. God raised this woman and sat her in the safety of what HE created. Did you get that? God did not allow

Deborah to sit in what man created. God created a PLACE for Deborah to do what He needed her to do. Man wasn't needed for this, no man could take credit, governance over, or claim to her assignment. I want to also mention this because we will talk about it a lot throughout this book. Her alignment, before God could employ her beneath that tree. Her alignment caused her to swiftly step into a position of authority Obedience births authority! Oftentimes, there is a look of authority, and the LOOK is too often mistaken for power. If there is ONLY a look, there is a breach of obedience. We can't just look the part! We must OBEY the Lord! We have to align to get access to authority. There must be an alignment before we access authority. Now, that means we must come into agreement with God, not with man. The man confirms what the Lord has spoken. So, we must come out of alignment with the covenants of men.

For clarification, we are men, and this has nothing to do with anyone else. Many times, we overlook the power of God because we're human. Our mindset can be a stumbling block. The Scriptures remind us that there's a path that seems right to us, but it only leads to ruin. Our ways have often hindered us from aligning with and agreeing with God. In our minds, we expect things to unfold in a specific manner, causing us to miss God's divine intervention because of our human limitations. We find ourselves questioning God, wondering how he could work through us, forgetting that he has been God for countless centuries—the eternal, self-existing one. We lose sight of his true nature and confine him within the limits of our understanding. Consequently, we resist aligning with him because we're preoccupied with figuring out the "how." Instead, we should focus on coming into alignment, minding our own business, and allowing him to manifest His nature in us. The reason is that Deborah was obedient and gained access to authority.

The other issue we have other than alignment is obeying while in place. We have an obedience problem. Deborah was able to do the things she did because she obeyed fearlessly. She didn't care who was uncomfortable. She wasn't concerned that God had told her right to send for a general. She wasn't concerned about what God had to say to the general. God gave her instructions, and she released them; she obeyed. We get challenged when it comes to following God because it puts us in an uncomfortable spot. Now, when I say "uncomfortable," I'm talking about our flesh acting all kinds of crazy and getting all worked up. God starts handing out assignments, decrees, and tasks, and we find ourselves getting all agitated and frustrated with the Almighty.

Take forgiveness, for instance. We're still wrestling with unforgiveness, even though God told us to forgive. The Holy Spirit gives us a clear directive, like rise and shine at 5:00 am to pray, but instead, we hit the snooze button and roll back into bed until 6:45, talking about, "Lord, I'm tired." God says, "Fast every Wednesday for six months," but our comeback is, "But Lord, you know the 4th of July is right around the corner, and that falls on a Wednesday. So, I might have to get back to you on that one." We've got to get real about following God's lead, no more excuses!

We don't understand why we don't have authority. We don't understand why we continue to get smacked by the enemy, but he's smacking us with our very own disobedience. Then we cry out to God like the children of Israel saying, "God save me. God help me." However, the reality is, what we're sitting in, we put ourselves there. "Well God, if those people at that church hadn't hurt me, I wouldn't be here. But the reality is if you hadn't let a human being become your God, you wouldn't be so hurt. Remember, fear might knock on the door, but faith is the one that answers. And as you continue to align, agree, and obey, you'll find that fear loses its grip on you, and faith becomes your guiding light.

Now, let's reflect on Deborah's journey. She wasn't exempt from fear or uncertainty. She wasn't immune to the challenges of her time. Yet, she chose alignment, agreement, and obedience despite the odds stacked against her. She didn't wait for fear to dissipate before she acted. Instead, she acted in faith, knowing that God's promises outweighed any fear or doubt.

So, what's holding you back? What fears are you allowing to dictate your actions or inactions? It's time to break free from the chains of fear and step boldly into alignment with God's will. Remember, God has not given you a spirit of fear but of power, love, and a sound mind (2 Timothy 1:7).

As you align, agree, and obey, you'll find yourself walking in the authority and power that God has ordained for you. You'll become a vessel through which God's victory, peace, and triumph are manifested in the world around you. So, embrace the journey, trust in God's guidance, and let go of fear. Your destiny awaits, and it's filled with purpose, authority, and divine alignment."

Closing Prayer

Father, I thank you God that you are calling your people in this hour to come into alignment, to agree with, and obey you, and Father I pray even now for the strength to align, agree, and obey and that we may come into authority in you. God, I pray that we are understanding and moving from a place of man's seat to being seated and exalted in high places. Father, I thank you God that your people are moving God from a place of fear to a place of authority coming into a place of God where they are judging the thing that held them captive and enslaved them. I decree that the Father is releasing you from that fear and is giving you the courage even now to do the very thing that you have been afraid to do. I decree that fear is broken off from your life in Jesus' name and you have the power, strength, and authority to align, agree, and obey God. Father, I thank you, that fear is broken off from the lives of your people in Jesus' name, Amen.

Chapter 3

Deborah the

Truth-Teller

In the preceding sections, we explored Deborah's roles as a patriot and a judge. Now, we delve into the core of Deborah as a woman anchored in truth. Before we can fully embody the roles of patriot, trailblazer, and judge, we must confront certain undeniable truths. While I was allowed to venture beyond the confines of the Book of Judges in earlier chapters, I was directed not to stray too far. Thus, we turn to the Gospel according to John. As John 8:32 states, "And you will know the truth, and the truth will liberate you." Additionally, John 16:13 confirms, "But when he, the Spirit of Truth, comes, he will guide you into all the truth." We now grasp that there were realms Deborah couldn't access without embracing and internalizing truth.

To serve as a judge, one must possess a profound understanding of truth, integrity, and discernment. It's impossible to justly judge without an intimate familiarity with truth. Your knowledge and comprehension of what is true must guide you in your role as a judge. Recall that Deborah, being a judge, had to discern and rightly judge matters brought before her. She had to recognize the essence of truth to make informed judgments.

Looking at the definition of "true" means "The quality or state of being accurate" or "In accordance with fact or reality" (Merriam-Webster's Collegiate Dictionary, 1999). Therefore, when we deal with the concept of truth, we're dealing with something we believe to be fact, reality, and something we've accepted. If we believe it to be fact in our reality and we've accepted it, then it becomes true to us.

In my contemplation before the Father, I realized one of the issues facing the body of Christ is our lack of understanding of the truth about who God is. We've been engaging in religious practices without truly grasping His nature. We worship and praise Him, but our lifestyles don't reflect a deep understanding of Him. If we fail to understand who He truly is, we cannot fully comprehend His desire for us.

Returning to John 8:32, let's focus on those initial six words: "And you will know the truth." Understanding "know" involves more than mere acquaintance; it requires awareness through observation, inquiry, and genuine connection. In our walk with God, we've accumulated a wealth of information, but some of it may not align with the truth. Certain notions we've accepted about God have led us away from genuine knowing and comprehension because they've been filtered through individuals who may not truly know Him themselves. Consequently, we've perpetuated misconceptions about God's true nature. We need to return to studying the Word for ourselves and seeking understanding directly from the Father.

We must get this right because God desires to bring us into a deeper understanding of who He is, but there's a level of truth we must embrace and walk in. There's an abandonment that must occur because many of us sense there must be more to God than what we've experienced. That sense is a sign that He's calling us into truth.

It's crucial to transition from passive engagement to active pursuit of truth. We must stop relying solely on the teachings of others and instead seek God directly. As 2 Timothy 2:15 says, "Study to show thyself approved unto God, a workman who needeth not to be ashamed, rightly dividing the word of truth." We must rightly divide the Word of truth and not limit ourselves to the teachings of man.

God is calling us to a deeper level of truth that will set us free from the cycles of lies and misconceptions. We must confront the lies within ourselves and the body of Christ. Truth is not meant to injure but to enlighten, heal, and liberate. As we embrace truth, we come into a deeper understanding of God's nature and our own identity in Him.

We become vessels of truth, detaching ourselves from the distractions of this world and leading others back to Him.

In this critical hour, God is raising individuals who will boldly pursue truth and challenge traditional practices and beliefs. These "divine detoxifiers" will lead others out of the intoxicating influence of lies and into the liberating truth of who God is. We must align ourselves with truth, both in our personal lives and in our service to others. As we embrace truth, we align with God's purpose and experience the freedom He offers. Let us be intentional about seeking and living in truth, for it is the foundation of our faith and the path to true transformation.

This quest for truth extends beyond personal matters; it encompasses our entire approach to life. We must not allow ourselves to be swayed by irrelevant concerns or superficial distractions. Our focus should not be on fleeting trends or empty pursuits that yield no godly fruit. Instead, we must prioritize truth, for it is the cornerstone of genuine transformation and empowerment.

As we align ourselves with truth, we gain clarity and insight into our purpose and identity. We shed the limitations imposed by falsehoods and misconceptions, and we step into the fullness of who God created us to be. This process requires courage and humility as we confront the lies within ourselves and the broader community of faith.

For too long, many have remained ensnared in cycles of deception and spiritual bondage. We have allowed fear, complacency, and the influence of others to hinder our pursuit of truth. But God is calling us to break free from these chains and embrace the truth that sets us free.

As individuals called to serve the body of Christ, we bear a solemn responsibility to lead others into truth. Whether as pastors, leaders, or ordinary believers, we must embody the principles of truth in our words and actions. We cannot shy away from confronting falsehoods or challenging prevailing norms if they contradict the truth of God's Word.

However, this must be done with love and compassion, not with condemnation or judgment. Just as Christ spoke truth to enlighten and heal, so too must we approach others with grace and understanding. We must be willing to listen, empathize, and walk alongside those who are struggling to break free from the grip of deception.

In this pursuit of truth, we may face opposition and resistance, both from within and from without. But we must remain steadfast, knowing that the truth we embrace is not our own, but God's truth. It is the light that exposes darkness, the freedom that breaks chains, and the hope that transforms lives.

As we continue this journey of truth, let us remember that our ultimate goal is not merely knowledge or enlightenment, but intimacy with the One who is the Truth. Let us seek Him earnestly, knowing that in His presence, we find the fullness of life and the assurance of our ultimate destiny.

May we, like Deborah, be willing to sit under the palm tree of truth, seeking wisdom and guidance from the Holy Spirit. May we be courageous in our pursuit of truth, uncompromising in our commitment to it, and unwavering in our faithfulness to God. And may we, through our words and actions, lead others into the liberating truth that sets hearts free and transforms lives.

Closing Prayer

Father, I thank you for another opportunity to serve your people. I pray that you continue to guide us, lead us, and give us the courage to come into truth so we can really see the truth of who you are. So, we see that you are our loving kind Father, not a tyrant. The truth that you don't want to just kill us and hurt us, but that you formed us, and you purposed us God. The truth that you only have good things in store for us God. The truth that you love us, Father. Give us the courage to know that you love us and that you are not an abusive parent God. Bring us into truth so we can move, operate, and live from the paradigm of truth and knowing that you love us. Christ death was for our salvation and for our access. Father, as we continue to move into truth God, move us into access. I pray that you awaken from your slumber and come into your place. Come into the knowledge of who he is. I command you now to awaken from your slumber because the Lord has need of you. Obey his voice and respond with yes. Father, I thank you that you have called us in this hour to do your bidding. The Father calls us to stand in obedience and power. Father, we love you we thank you we bless you in Jesus' name, Amen.

Chapter 4

Deborah the Warrior

Walk with me as we journey through the life of Deborah, a trailblazer of her time. In our first chapter, we delved into the core of Deborah, our patriotic sister. We unearthed her divine calling as a judge, recognizing her unwavering commitment to truth and obedience to God. Now, I am thrilled to unveil the revelation bestowed upon me regarding Deborah, our courageous warrior. Let us proceed, guided step by step by the Almighty.

In Judges 4:6-9, we witness Deborah's divine authority as she commands Barak to lead the army against Sisera. She demonstrates her strategic prowess, guiding Barak with confidence born from her experience and God-given insight. As a ranking warrior, Deborah sends word to Barak, a high-ranking general, showcasing her authority and influence.

A strategist as well as a warrior, Deborah provides Barak with precise instructions and divine strategy, ensuring victory against overwhelming odds. She stands firm in her authority, possessing the foresight to surrender them to him because she already held possession in the realm of the spirit. Her authority is not for self-glorification but to be a vessel through which God's power flows.

Deborah's encounter with Barak reflects her unyielding confidence in God's word, regardless of societal norms. In an era where women were marginalized, Deborah boldly commands respect and authority, transcending gender barriers to fulfill her divine purpose. Barak's humility in acknowledging her authority underscores the significance of obedience over pride. Pride, a deadly adversary, often blinds us to God's commands and obstructs His victories. Deborah's example teaches us to cast aside pride and embrace humility, recognizing that victory belongs to God alone.

As warriors of the Kingdom, we must confront pride daily, surrendering ourselves completely to God's will. In the battlefield of faith, pride must be vanquished for God's power to reign supreme. Let us heed Deborah's call to humility, abandoning our prideful inclinations and yielding wholeheartedly to God's divine authority. As warriors of honor, we must eradicate pride from our lives, surrendering to God's transformative fire and embracing His victory. May we walk in humility and courage, knowing that our strength lies in God alone.

Deborah's unwavering resolve to stand in her authority, despite societal expectations, serves as a beacon for us all. She did not shrink back in the face of adversity but boldly proclaimed God's word, regardless of the consequences. Her example challenges us to relinquish our fears and insecurities, trusting in God's guidance and provision.

As warriors in the Kingdom of God, we must emulate Deborah's courage and steadfastness, refusing to be swayed by the opinions of others. Our allegiance lies solely with our Commander, and we must be willing to follow His lead, even when it means standing alone against the tide of popular opinion. Pride, the insidious enemy within, seeks to exalt itself above God's authority, leading us astray from His divine purpose. Deborah's humility and obedience serve as a stark contrast to the pitfalls of pride, reminding us of the importance of submission and surrender to God's will.

Let us heed Deborah's call to arms, embracing our roles as fearless warriors in God's army. May we lay down our pride and ego at the feet of our Commander, trusting in His wisdom and guidance to lead us to victory? As we march forward in faith, may we stand firm in our authority, knowing that God goes before us, paving the way for triumph and glory.

Closing Prayer

Father, we bless you. We love you and we thank you, God. We thank you. Father, we bless you. We love you thank you. God thank you. Thank you for the warrior awakening. They are warriors. Awakening the warrior. Speaking the warrior. Living the warrior. Breathing the warrior. Father, I thank you that she is awakening, that he is awakening. Thank you, God, for overturning orders and issuing orders in the kingdoms of heaven and ports of heaven. God bless you. Bless your people and God continue to give us the courage to war on your behalf. Thank you that our families will be saved. Our generations will be restored because we honor you, Father. We bless you and we love you in Jesus' name, Amen.

Chapter 5

Deborah the Ruler

We've delved into the depths of Deborah's warrior spirit, but how does she embody the essence of leadership? First, let's explore what it means to be a leader. A leader exercises authority and dominion. Synonymous with the concept of a leader is a ruler—a figure vested with authority, dominion, and governance. Thus, when we speak of someone with authority or dominion, we're referring to a ruler.

We've established that Deborah was appointed as a prophet during a pivotal period in Israel's history. Even from this perspective, she held a certain level of authority and dominion. However, her authority wasn't derived from earthly kingdoms but from her position in the kingdom of

God—a realm we uncovered in Deborah the Warrior. As we journey through this exploration, let's revisit Judges 4:4 and examine the first characteristic: courage. Deborah exemplified courage; an essential trait for leaders and rulers alike. Deborah's calling came during a challenging time for Israel—captivity under the oppression of their enemies. God called her to lead amidst adversity, and she responded with bravery and unwavering confidence.

Despite the unpopularity of her call and the disobedience of the people she served, Deborah stepped forward boldly, ready to fulfill God's purpose. Consider your own life. Perhaps God called you during times of hardship, and oppression, or when it seemed unpopular to answer His call.

True calling isn't always accompanied by popularity; rather, it demands courage and obedience. Deborah's example teaches us that God doesn't choose the perfect; He selects the courageous who are willing to carry out His work. In Judges 4:1-4, we witness Israel's cry for deliverance, which prompted God to raise Deborah. This illustrates that leadership requires courage, especially during times of adversity. When God calls, we mustn't be concerned about the outcome but trust in His guidance. Deborah's leadership was characterized by wisdom and active listening—a quality often overlooked in today's leaders. She didn't merely listen to respond but sought to understand, gaining wisdom and knowledge in the process. In our era of rampant speaking but limited listening, Deborah's example reminds us of the power of attentive ears and discerning spirits.

The Bible urges us to be quick to hear and slow to speak (James 1:19). In a time where many are eager to share their words but few listen, Deborah's attentive listening sets a valuable precedent. When we cultivate a spirit of attentiveness in God's presence, we position ourselves to receive divine wisdom and guidance. Deborah's life underscores the importance of humility in leadership. Despite her authority and influence, she remained humble, acknowledging God's role in her victories. Her humility paved the way for trust and respect among the people she led.

As leaders, we must emulate Deborah's humility, recognizing that our authority comes from God, not ourselves. Deborah's confidence stemmed not from herself but from her unwavering faith in God. Leaders take note: true confidence comes from knowing and trusting in God, not from our abilities. When we place our confidence in God, we become vessels for His power and authority. Lastly, Deborah's directness in delivering God's message highlights the necessity of clarity and conviction in leadership. She didn't compromise or sugarcoat God's word but spoke it boldly and without reservation. Leaders today must likewise be direct in conveying God's truth, not swayed by fear or concern for perception. Deborah epitomizes the qualities of a true leader—courageous, wise, humble, and confident in God's power.

As we aspire to lead, let us draw inspiration from her example, seeking to emulate her faithfulness and obedience. In doing so, we fulfill God's calling and bring glory to His name. When the path ahead seems obscured, may divine illumination guide your way. Rise, child of God, and step into the authority bestowed upon you. This is your divine inheritance, your birthright as a child of the Most High. Do not shrink back in the face of adversity, for the Lord your God goes before you. He has equipped you with all you need to fulfill the purpose He has ordained for your life. Trust in His provision, lean not on your understanding, and acknowledge Him in all your ways.

As you journey forward, remember the example set by Deborah, the ruler and leader chosen by God. Let her life inspire you to walk boldly in your calling, to listen attentively to the voice of the Lord, and to lead with humility and wisdom. May your words carry the weight of truth, your actions reflect the character of Christ, and your life shine as a beacon of hope to those around you. Go forth in the strength of the Lord, for He is with you always. In His service, you will find fulfillment, purpose, and joy beyond measure. So, rise, O ruler, and take your place in the kingdom of God. The world awaits the manifestation of the sons and daughters of God, and you are called to lead the way.

With faith as your shield and the Word of God as your sword, march forward into the destiny that awaits you.

For in His presence, there is fullness of joy, and at His right hand, there are pleasures forevermore. Therefore, let us press on toward the goal of the prize of the upward call of God in Christ Jesus. For He who has called you is faithful, and He will surely accomplish all that He has promised. So, rise, Deborah, rise, ruler, rise, leader. For the time is now, and the world is waiting for you to shine. Go forth in the power of the Holy Spirit, and let your light so shine before men that they may see your good works and glorify your Father in heaven. This is your moment, your season, your time to rise and reign with Christ. So, step into your authority, walk in obedience, and fulfill the purpose for which you were created. For you are called, chosen, and anointed by God Almighty.

Arise, O Deborah, arise, ruler, arise, leader. For such a time as this, you have been raised to make a difference in the world. So, go forth with confidence, go forth with courage, go forth with conviction. For the Lord your God is with you, and He will never leave you nor forsake you. Now is the time to rise and shine, for the glory of the Lord is upon you. Let your light so shine before men that they may see your good works and glorify your Father in heaven. This is your moment, your destiny, your divine appointment. So, rise, Deborah, rise, ruler, rise, leader, and take your place in the kingdom of God. Amen.

Closing Prayer

Father, I pray that you strengthen and bless your people. I pray that you heal every broken place that keeps us from obeying your orders and keeps us scared. Father, I pray that people come into complete compliance and alignment with your word concerning them because you are our ruler. Father, may we accept your lordship and leadership in our lives. Forgive us where we've compromised and bowed our knees to an idol because of fear of being judged, thrown away, rejected, pushed aside, and unseen. God, forgive us for bowing our knees to the idols that have caused us to abandon who you said we are. Now I pray to God for courage, embrace it, be okay with it, and love it. Father, we appreciate you in Jesus' name, Amen.

Chapter 6

Deborah the Prophetess

In the journey of understanding the prophetic mantle, let's delve into the life of Deborah, the prophetess, as portrayed in Judges 4:4. Here, we witness Deborah stepping into her prophetic role at a crucial juncture in Israel's history. The Scriptures describe her as not just a casual observer but as a leader, fully immersed in guiding Israel through tumultuous times. The call to prophethood isn't a trivial matter. Like all divine appointments, it comes with prerequisites and demands a deep understanding of God's will. In our era, there's a palpable hunger for the prophetic, often overshadowed by the desire for recognition or popularity. However, the prophet's mantle isn't about seeking the spotlight, but about embracing the weighty responsibilities it entails.

The essence of the prophet's call extends far beyond merely foretelling the future. It's about embodying the character of God, walking in His ways, and discerning His voice amidst the noise of the world. Deborah exemplified this by not only prophesying but also by judging and leading according to the Holy Spirit's guidance.

Five pivotal roles define the prophet's mission, all rooted in the character of God. The prophet is called to pull down, dismantle ungodly strongholds, and usher in God's authority. This role requires discernment and a keen awareness of spiritual realities. Next comes the task of destruction, where the prophet confronts and nullifies the works of darkness. Elijah's confrontation with the prophets of Baal illustrates this vividly, showing how the prophet stands boldly against all that opposes God's truth. After pulling down and destroying, the prophet casts down, releasing individuals from the burdens and hindrances they carry. This act of divine intervention, guided by the Spirit, leads to liberation and breakthrough in the lives of God's people.

The final two roles, building, and planting, demonstrate the prophet's commitment to restoration and establishment. Just as Elijah brought rain after the drought, the prophet brings forth growth and stability in the lives they touch. Yet, this calling isn't for the faint of heart or the self-seeking. It demands total surrender and a willingness to lay down one's life for the cause. Those who covet this mantle without understanding its weight risk grave consequences.

In our pursuit of the prophetic, let's remember that true prophets are characterized by humility, integrity, and an unwavering commitment to God's truth. They don't seek accolades or material gain but are solely focused on fulfilling God's purposes. As we navigate this journey, may we seek the heart of God above all else, knowing that He alone equips and empowers us for every task He calls us to. Let's embrace the prophetic call with reverence, humility, and a burning passion to see His kingdom come on earth as it is in heaven. Prophetess Deborah serves as a profound example of a leader who embodied the character of God and fulfilled her prophetic calling with courage and integrity. She didn't seek fame or accolades but faithfully carried out her duties, leading Israel with wisdom and discernment.

Like Deborah, modern-day prophets should prioritize aligning themselves with God's character rather than seeking personal gain or recognition. They should be unyielding in their commitment to speak God's truth, even when it's uncomfortable or unpopular. Furthermore, Deborah's multifaceted role illustrates that the prophetic calling involves more than just foretelling the future. It encompasses judging, counseling, guiding, and interceding for God's people. This comprehensive understanding of the prophetic underscores the importance of humility, prayerfulness, and obedience for those who claim to be prophets.

Ultimately, as we reflect on the life and ministry of Prophetess Deborah, we're reminded of the profound responsibility that comes with the prophetic calling. It's not a title to be coveted or pursued for personal gain but a sacred duty to faithfully represent God's character and lead His people according to His will.

Closing Prayer

Father, we bless you and we thank you for another opportunity to serve your people. God, I thank you for clarifying and making plain what you have mandated for the prophets and what you've mandated them for them to carry. They should have your character, Father. I pray that you begin to deliver and heal those of us God who have been called to this office; those who have lusted and coveted this office. Father, I pray that you're delivering and healing hands begin to touch your people. God, I pray that you will cause us to come into compliance and alignment with what you've called us to do, even if it's not this. Father, I thank you God for those of us who have been called to this. Thank you for choosing us, giving us the strength of tenacity, courage to pursue you, and your character so that when we stand before the people, they see you and not us. I pray God that you deliver and save the false prophets that stand in your name, but God knows that knows you not. Father, even now we repent on their behalf, God. We pray to God that salvation and deliverance come to them in the name of Jesus. Father, we love you and we bless you in Jesus' name, Amen.

Chapter 7

Deborah the Agitator

In contemplating the role of Deborah as an agitator, I've been profoundly struck by the necessity of yielding to God's sovereignty. The Lord continually reminds me of the paramount importance of relying on Him. No amount of skill or training can compare to the posture of learning and depending on God. My earnest prayer tonight is that you grasp the Father's message and that it propels you to trust and depend on Him even more. On our own, we cannot fulfill God's calling; we need Him. He's not merely essential; He's everything. In my view, He's the sole necessity because, with Him, He directs us to where we ought to be. Amen.

Now, let's delve into what defines an agitator. An agitator is characterized as someone who urges others to protest or rebel against what is wrong. Synonymous terms for agitator include troublemaker or rouser. So, when we encounter an agitator, we engage with someone who prompts others to protest and rebel against injustice. While we might sometimes perceive agitators in a negative light, the Lord has revealed to me that being called by God to serve in any capacity often entails the ability to agitate certain aspects of our surroundings.

Deborah, a passionate woman, was raised and empowered by God to agitate and lead Israel into war. As we've witnessed in preceding chapters, God called her in response to the people's cries of oppression. Often, the awakening of the agitator occurs when something is amiss in a situation. When God takes you to places and positions where your mere presence causes agitation, it signifies a divine intervention. Consequently, when God sends in someone who has answered His call, that individual begins to discern through the Spirit what's amiss, leading to agitation.

I've discovered from personal experience that God sometimes permits irritations and agitation to prompt our growth and expansion. When the agitator emerges, we're awakened to discomfort and disturbance. Oftentimes, our complacency and passivity compel God to stir and agitate us to make us grow and progress.

God sends troublemakers because they refuse to conform; they reject aligning with the status quo. They defy systems and structures that lack divine authority, challenging anything that bears God's name without His true endorsement. Therefore, when God dispatches the agitator, a sense of unrest permeates the atmosphere, signaling that something isn't right.

Have you ever entered a situation and sensed that everything was unraveling? People begin to act erratically, and order starts to disintegrate. It's because an agitator, representing the character of God, has entered the scene, stirring up disruption. The agitator functions as a divine stirring device, challenging us to confront injustice and disorder.

However, embracing the role of an agitator isn't about seeking conflict or causing chaos. Instead, it's about embodying the character of God and allowing His presence within us to naturally provoke change. The agitator operates not from a place of self-interest but from a deep commitment to aligning with God's truth and justice.

Deborah's agitation for change and deliverance brought about the zeal needed for battle. Her passion and refusal to compromise inspired Barak and the armies of God to fight. Before experiencing victory, they had to withstand the agitation. Yet, too often, we miss God because we cannot endure the discomfort of agitation.
Just as the soil must be disturbed before planting, our lives sometimes need agitation to facilitate growth and purification. The agitator doesn't deal with surface issues but delves deep into our fears, insecurities, and hang-ups. They prompt us to confront the truth and repent of our sins, injustices, and lies.

In moments of turmoil, when deep-seated emotions bubble up, we're compelled to recognize our reliance on

God and acknowledge the bitterness, envy, and resentment within us. The agitator speaks the truth, revealing the roots of our authenticity and challenging us to address unhealed wounds.

God dispatches agitators to reset and reprogram us, wiping away dysfunctional systems and patterns so that we can function properly. Yet, many resist the agitation, fearing discomfort and change. However, resistance only prolongs our growth and delays our destiny.

As the Earth groans for the revelation of the sons of God, we must embrace the role of agitators, allowing God to agitate our spirits and transform us from within. Only then can we effectively fulfill our purpose and become instruments of change in the hands of the Almighty.

At Truth Church, I consistently remind the congregation that when issues rise to the surface, they are on their way out. It's a process of resolution initiated by God Himself. I've surrendered to God's rightful place in my life, removing any barriers that might hinder our relationship. I refuse to overlook any aspect of His glory, and I refuse to allow external forces to lead me astray. When agitators arise, I see them not as enemies but as catalysts for growth—a sign that God intends to fortify and empower me. I embrace these moments, determined not to be swayed from my alignment with Him.

We must recognize that not everyone experiences agitation, so when it comes, we must give glory to God, understanding it as His invitation to transformation. I encourage you to embrace the role of the agitator in your own life, allowing God to stir and challenge you to greater heights. Let us not be consumed by distractions but be consumed by God and His purposes. When we focus on being the church, we become unshakeable and unmovable, fully aligned with His will.

So, my brothers and sisters, let us welcome the agitation, for in it lies the invitation to profound growth and transformation. Let us be agents of change, embodying the character of God and allowing His presence to work in and through us. May we be steadfast in our commitment to Him, refusing to be swayed by external forces or distractions. May we always give glory to God for His transformative work in our lives. I pray that this message has stirred something within you, igniting a passion to embrace the role of the agitator and to fully surrender to God's transformative power. May you walk in alignment with His will, fully empowered to fulfill your divine purpose. Amen.

Closing Prayer

I pray that the power, anointing, and weight of God rest upon you and that you truly come into your sonship and understand how much he loves you. I pray you understand how much he wants you. He didn't just call you, but he chose you. A lot of people missed the chosen part because they resisted the agitation. So, embrace the agitation. Embrace the growth. I pray that you will be strengthened. Father, bless your people. God calls all of us to embrace the agitation that you send into our lives to help us grow, increase, and strengthen us so we can look more like you. So, we can become Christ beings because we understand that this is a continual work, and our perfection is only in you. Father, I thank you God that your people are strengthened, and that your people trust you enough to allow the agitation to come. God, I thank you that we are coming into a place growing into full-blown trees and not just specs of branches on the ground. Father, I thank you even now that albeit that the ax is laid at the root of the tree, that we will bear fruit and that your name will be glorified in our lives. Father, we bless you and we honor you in Jesus' name, Amen.

Chapter 8

Deborah the Wife

As we continue our exploration of the multifaceted persona of the prophetess Deborah, let us now direct our attention to her role as a wife. While the Scriptures offer scant details about her marital status, Judges 4:4 notably identifies her as "the wife of Lappidoth." The name "Lappidoth" holds profound symbolism, meaning "torch" or "lightning" in Hebrew. This illuminates Deborah's character, portraying her as a beacon of light and fire. She wasn't merely a summoned woman of God; she was divinely called to embody light and fire within the context of marriage.

Delving deeper, we encounter a woman ablaze with passion and purpose. Yet, in our modern era, the significance of the journey into marriage often gets overshadowed by the allure of the wedding day. We become enamored with the festivities while overlooking the profound preparation required for a lifelong partnership. The prevailing narrative of the independent woman poses a challenge, leading many to approach God with a mindset of self-sufficiency rather than reliance. We've embraced a culture of self-empowerment, yet true strength lies in acknowledging our dependence on divine guidance.

Submission, often misunderstood as weakness, is, in truth, a display of strength — a willingness to yield to a higher authority. It entails embracing a divine order, whether in marriage or our relationship with God. However, societal misconceptions often propagate the notion that submission equates to inferiority, particularly within religious contexts. Finding a life partner, as Proverbs 18:22 suggests, involves recognizing more than just a companion; it's about identifying someone who embodies the qualities of a virtuous partner. This realization prompts us to reevaluate our approach to relationships, transcending superficial desires to embrace the essence of partnership.

The Proverbs 31 woman serves as an exemplar, embodying traits of nobility, trustworthiness, and diligence. She isn't merely a homemaker; she's a partner in every aspect of life. Her capacity extends beyond personal independence; she dedicates herself to fulfilling the responsibilities of marriage and beyond. In our quest for partnership, we must shed the baggage of past relationships and seek divine guidance in selecting a life companion. Settling for potential often leads to heartache; instead, we must align ourselves with God's plan, trusting that He knows what's best for us. Ultimately, the journey of marriage is a sacred covenant, a lifelong commitment that demands dedication and humility. As wives, we honor our husbands not by exerting control but by offering support and encouragement. We relinquish the need for dominance and embrace the divine order, trusting that God's plan transcends our desires.

As for the journey ahead, uncertainties may loom, but I hold steadfast to my faith. I trust in God and His plan. I submitted to His will, and He blessed me with a remarkable man — imperfect yet perfectly suited for me. Now, let's address the topic of submission, often regarded as contentious. Many perceive it as a display of weakness, but I disagree. Submission is a testament to strength. It involves acknowledging God's divine order and placing our trust in His wisdom. It's not about blindly obeying; it's about aligning ourselves with His plan, even in the face of adversity.

In marriage, submission is a partnership — a graceful dance between two souls in harmony with each other and with God. It's rooted in mutual respect, honor, and love. I submit to my husband because I respect him, honor him, and love him deeply. And you know what? He reciprocates in kind. But let's dispel any misconceptions. Submission doesn't entail losing our identity or silencing our voices. It doesn't relegate us to the role of doormats or second-class citizens. Rather, it empowers us to become stronger together, united in purpose and vision. It fosters an environment where we lift each other, support each other's aspirations, and grow together in love and understanding.

So, my dear sisters, let's embrace our roles as wives with joy and gratitude. Let's honor our husbands, uplift them, and pray for them earnestly. Let's lay the foundation of our homes on pillars of love, trust, and unwavering faith. Above all, let's entrust our marriages to God's divine plan, knowing that He walks with us, guiding us every step of the way.

Closing Prayer

I pray that you are strengthened and blessed. I pray that you are blessed. Father, bless your people. Strengthen us, God. Thank you for correcting us. Thank you, God, for bringing us into more understanding of what you call and define as a wife. Help us to be of help to you on Earth and if you desire, help us to help our husbands, and not a hindrance. Forgive us, God, for the areas where we've hindered our husbands and we've hindered your moves because of our disobedience and our issues. Strengthen us and have mercy on us God. Jesus' name, Amen.

Chapter 9

Deborah the Mother

As we journey through the rich tapestry of the life of our esteemed sister prophet Deborah, it has been a profound blessing to my spirit, and I trust it has resonated with each of you as well. While in deep communion with the Almighty, seeking His guidance on what He wished to impart, my attention was directed to Judges 5:7. In the amplified version, it proclaims, "The villagers ceased to be; they ceased in Israel until I, Deborah, arose, until I arose, a mother in Israel." As we prepare to delve into the revelation of Deborah as a mother, let's ensure we have our definitions clear.

I delved into the meanings of motherhood, which, of course, encompass the typical aspects like giving birth, adopting, nurturing a child, and being a female ancestor.

However, it was the subsequent definition that stirred my soul: "a woman who holds a position of authority or responsibility." Let's meditate on that, my sisters, and invite the Holy Spirit to illuminate the power and authority that accompany women in positions of influence.

When we think of a mother, we often envision a woman giving birth or raising children, right? Well, in Judges 4, there is no mention that Deborah had her children. It simply states that she was a wife. Yet, when Israel was in dire straits in chapter 4 and a cry for help resounded, guess whom God sent to deliver them? The unlikely candidate – Deborah. And as I continued reading, I saw it: Deborah epitomized that maternal instinct. You know how it is when our children, not just the ones we gave birth to, but our beloved ones, encounter trouble. There's a snap, a call to action, and we're ready to move mountains for our beloved. So, when a cry went out, up rose the prophet – the Mother.

Fast forward to chapter five, and there's Deborah, singing and worshiping. She recounts how the village lay in ruins, and things did not improve until she stepped up.

Biblically, there is no record that Deborah had her children, yet in verse seven of chapter five, she declares herself the mother of Israel. Sometimes, we disqualify women from motherhood because they cannot physically give birth or circumstances force them to give up their children. But in those moments, we overlook the fact that these circumstances do not alter who you are. Regardless of what happens, you're still a Mother. Bear with me as I explain further.

Deborah's narrative teaches us that motherhood transcends mere biological or physical aspects. It embodies an outward expression of embracing matters of the heart. Yes, it's a natural inclination that emanates from within us. Mothers are nurturers and protectors, and, in the scriptures, Deborah began to manifest these traits that were inherent within her. So, here's the message, especially for the Mothers out there – circumstances do not define who you are. You are still a Mother, and that's a potent truth.

When Deborah emerged from beneath that tree, she did so with a divine purpose, a steadfast resolve, a God-given mission. The Almighty beckoned to her, and she, a daughter of the Most High, responded with obedience. Yet, her authority did not just surface; it surged within her as she heard the cries of her child, her nation—Israel. Mother went into defense mode; a protective stance innates to mothers. She sought the Lord's counsel to emancipate her child from the clutches of adversity. Stepping out from the shade of the palm tree and the comfort it provided, Mother accessed divine strategies to ensure her child's deliverance. Every woman, whether through childbirth or love and relationships, encounters a pivotal moment. A cry echoes from her past, propelling her into the role of strategist, defender, and protector.

There comes a time when Mother must rise, casting aside the cloak of comfort, as her children, her nation, cry out. Understand, that there is a nation within her, a divine trust to nurture, protect, and defend. In this critical era, mothers must arise, rousing from the slumber of comfort to answer the cries of their babies. Whether it's that wayward child, a neglected ministry, or a dormant business, each holds the seed of a nation entrusted by God. Mother, you do not need permission; you possess inherent authority.

Deborah, as a mother, rose with complete jurisdiction, not seeking validation from external sources. So, Mother, rise unapologetically, for your authority extends beyond mere permission. In the scriptures, Deborah, as a mother, rose with undeniable authority over Israel, exemplifying that maternal jurisdiction does not hinge on permission. Mothers, both in the natural and the spiritual, resonate with a shared sentiment: you can tamper with many things, but do not touch your babies. It's a universal truth, transcending cultural boundaries. Recognize that our roles extend beyond biological children to encompass birthing the spiritual destinies and purposes God has assigned us. Let us break free from the chains of delay and deliver the promises that have long been held hostage within us.

We are way past our due dates, birthing purpose and destiny. We're gripping destiny, making it our top priority. Why? Firstly, we doubt ourselves; we feel inadequate. Secondly, we are concerned about others' opinions. We must break free from seeking human approval for what we are inherently capable of. Imagine, no birthing pools, no doctors—our bodies are inherently designed by God for unassisted birth. We're rejecting the natural order, thinking it should conform to societal expectations. The midwife, at times, only coaches, not forcefully altering what our bodies naturally do. We have lost sight of our innate abilities.

Mother, ask yourself: What are you willing to fight for? Often, we passionately discuss defending our purpose and destiny, our babies. We must decide what we are willing to fight for. We've lost sight of the spiritual warfare—bigger than what's visible. There are nations within you, woman. A biblical example: a woman pregnant with twins, nations wrestling within her. We need to shift from fighting against God to fighting against the enemy. Stop fighting each other; instead, confront the devil. We must unite against him, for he will retreat when faced with a collective force of empowered mothers.

Amid the battle, God invites us to a place of peace, like a palm tree oasis. In that serene space, we find the courage to hear His voice and accept His words. Peace and stillness give birth to bravery and confidence. Shedding insecurity, we embrace God's perspective, perfecting what concerns us. When we accept His words, we walk away from insecurity. Now, having heard God's voice and accepted His view of us, we wield authority and jurisdiction—protecting our babies. We understand that, through His voice and acceptance, we are enough. He wants me and I am good enough as is. What needs to be changed concerning me, he'll do it in his time.

God understands that I've walked a path where certain choices and circumstances shaped my journey, yet they don't define or redefine the purpose He has for me. Now, beneath the comforting shade of this palm tree, I find solace in God's peace. I'm learning to fully embrace the identity He has called me to, basking in the protection of His covering. Mother, it's crucial to remember we're not alone in this journey.

When we enter a space of peace with God, embracing our authority and operating within our jurisdiction, we discover that heaven supports us. Failure becomes a non-option, just like when Deborah, as a Mother, exercised her authority, seeking reinforcements to protect her crying child. As we accept our authority and embrace our jurisdiction, we gain influence. In places where we'd normally struggle, we can make a simple call to get things resolved. We've tapped into God's peace and received His guidance, and now it's time to execute. Our babies are still crying, and we've submitted our issues to God, receiving strategies and understanding. We can call in specialists, armed with the skills needed to address the situation because we've embraced our authority.

In moments of uncertainty and doubt, we must recall what we're fighting for. The enemy is attempting to wipe out a whole generation, targeting our children, grandchildren, nieces, nephews, and even great-grandchildren. It's not because of our past sins; it's an attack on the potential impact this generation will have. Mother, the devil attacks what poses a threat, and that includes the nation birthed through us. We are not just former this or that; we were chosen vessels to bring forth a nation with a divine purpose.

It's time to shift from living vicariously through our children to understanding that God used us for a purpose. We don't have to control everything or compete with our children. Instead, by embracing our authority and purpose, we become supporters, applauding their success. When we fully embrace who God says we are, we can push and give birth to the nation He placed within us. No longer afraid of our nation surpassing us, we pray with belief, knowing that our nation will prosper and fulfill the purpose God has ordained. Often, we miss it when God is at work; we become entangled because we're scared, trying to control everything. Mother, it's time to release that control, let it go, push it out. Relinquish control, let go, let go, so God can work through what you've brought into the world, what you've carried.

We limit ourselves to our experiences, but it takes courage, my dear sisters. Like how God had Deborah sit under the tree, a symbol of His presence and coverage. She gained confidence and courage there. When it was time to rise, she did so fearlessly, understanding the assignment. Before Deborah arose, the place was desolate, in torment. Mother, remember what you're fighting for. Get up, Mother, you're fighting for nations, for those bearing your mark, your name. There's a cry in the land, and it won't stop until you arrive. It's not just about ministry; it's about embracing your authority in God. You're still a Mother, a woman with authority, whether you struggled with addiction or made mistakes. Rise, Mother, the nation is crying, and you have the authority and jurisdiction given by God.

You don't stop being a Mother because circumstances dictate otherwise. You are good enough, always have been. It doesn't matter what happened then; we're talking about now. Arise, Mother, and as you move forward, comforted by God, victory is guaranteed. Deborah arose, heard the cry, received strategy from the Father, called skilled reinforcements, and God gave her victory. So, Mother, stop being scared; victory is certain. Understand your authority and your jurisdiction. You have authority over what you've given birth to; start speaking and decreeing over them. Whether it's a failing business, a troubled child, or a seemingly dead vision, prophesy, speaks life.

Mother, you have authority; the enemy doesn't know what to do with a Mother who understands her authority. Pray, prophesy, and speak the Word of God over your nations. It's time to arise, Mother because the earth is waiting for you. Lock arms with other Mothers, fight together, and you'll see nations birthed, visions fulfilled, and destinies realized. Arise, Mother, you've got this, and we're waiting to see what you birth next. I pray for our strength to be renewed. Take charge of this liberation; let it be more than a fleeting moment. Embrace it fully, and rise. Reach out to your sisters and connect with them. Transform this into a consistent practice, applying it to your life.

As you rise, remember to uplift others—bring Mother along with you. While God is lifting us, extend your hand to pull someone else up with you. My prayer is that you find strength and blessings in abundance tonight. May the Lord God empower all of us to rise, and may this elevated state become a permanent posture. Let it not be a temporary feeling but a steadfast position that we maintain. Yes, like Deborah, rise without seeking permission; stand firmly in your authority. Mother rises, and I ask for God's blessing upon us. We express gratitude to God for another opportunity to share His work with His people.

Closing Prayer

Father, we pray to God for all the women and men of God. Father, I pray that we arise and take our authority and our jurisdiction. Father calls us to walk into a place of victory that we have not known, and we decree even now that not another one of our sons and daughters, destiny, or purpose will be lost. We stand tonight and we will arise, God, we will rise to the occasion. So, Father, I bless you that you are meeting every need and standing in every courtroom, every home, every cell, and every job. God, I pray you are standing in the places where we need you to be in this moment. We bless you and we honor you. We pray for every purpose, every destiny, every plan, every business, every idea, and every book that we have been afraid to pursue. We declare victory and we demand and decree that we will arise. Father, we bless you now. We love you. we thank you, in Jesus' name, Amen.

Chapter 10

Deborah the Poet

Let's delve into the captivating narrative of Deborah the poet. When we ponder upon poetry and its intersection with the divine word, it evokes a multitude of reflections. However, what truly intrigues me is exploring the essence of poetry across various languages and cultures—what lies at its core, you know? We're all familiar with the fundamental definition of a poet: someone endowed with that ineffable ability to articulate thoughts and imagination. Let me quickly reference the textbook definition just to ensure we're aligned. But when I envision a poet, I see someone who possesses a fluidity of expression and depth of reasoning. I regard rappers as poets. When I think of poets, I imagine individuals weaving intricate lines, crafting rhymes, and dropping bars, as my son would say.

Now, let's journey to Judges 5, where profound verses are sung in honor of the Almighty. Picture this: following a victorious battle, God calls upon Israel once more for triumph. And who answers the call? Prophetess Deborah, laying down verses for the Divine. Yes, Prophetess Deborah and General Barak, pouring out their hearts in song before the Lord. Amen to that! So, when faced with such moments, let's explore Judges 5:1-5 for insights on navigating these junctures. Allow me to share a snippet, to keep us focused, okay? Let's gracefully tread the path guided by the Lord as we unravel this together.

Judges 5:1-5 reads, "On that day Deborah and Barak son of Abinoam sang this song: 'When the princes in Israel take the lead, when the people willingly offer themselves—praise the Lord! Hear this, you kings! Listen, you rulers! I, even I, will sing to the Lord; I will praise the Lord, the God of Israel, in song. When you, Lord, went out from Seir, when you marched from the land of Edom, the earth shook, the heavens poured, and the clouds poured down water. The mountains quaked before the Lord, the One of Sinai, before the Lord, the God of Israel" (NIV). In dissecting this verse,

Deborah initiates the song by evoking the might, wonder, and reverence for the Lord. Her focus is on the opening words of verse 2, addressing the role of leaders, particularly princesses, who wield authority. Deborah underscores the significance of leaders, emphasizing that when those in authority, such as princesses in Israel, lead in worship, and people willingly offer praise, it invokes divine reverence.

Expanding upon our previous discourse on motherhood and authority, Judges 5 shifts the narrative to Deborah exemplifying the impact when leaders and those in authority wholeheartedly devote themselves to praising the Lord. To provide clarity, let's briefly explore the term "poet." A poet, as traditionally defined, possesses exceptional abilities in perceiving and expressing beauty and lyricism. Delving deeper, a poet is someone endowed with special imaginative and expressive powers—indicating a position of authority.

Transitioning to Judges 5, we witness the prophetess, judge, and general, Deborah, engaging in a song of praise to the Lord. The biblical understanding of poetry in ancient Hebrew aligns it with a sacred song or chant, as evidenced in Exodus 15:1-9 or Numbers 21:17-20. Therefore, Deborah's song is a poetic expression, a heartfelt melody sung unto the Lord. What distinguishes Judges 5 is the instructional aspect embedded within Deborah's song. She highlights the transformative power when women in authority, the princesses of Israel, assume leadership roles.

Deborah encourages wise women to embrace their authority, stressing that when leaders take their rightful place, and people willingly offer praise, a unique and elevated spiritual realm is accessed. In essence, Judges 5 presents a profound illustration of the convergence of authority and worship, urging women in leadership positions to recognize the sacred duty that comes with their roles and to lead with wisdom and reverence, contributing to a harmonious symphony of praise. When we embrace our authority, even in the context of praising and worship, we enter a profound understanding of our identity. It is at this point that we realize our capacity to lead. As poets, what we do extends beyond words; we become leaders guiding others into worship. This leadership involves inspiring those under our authority to join in praise and song. The essence of this leadership is captured in the opening lines of verse 2: "When the princes in Israel take the lead, when the people willingly offer themselves—praise to the Lord" (NIV). Thus, by taking the initiative to sing praises to the Lord, those under our influence willingly and freely join in, recognizing our leadership.

Moving on to verse 3, the message is directed towards kings and rulers, continuing the dialogue with those in positions of authority. As poets, our unique power lies in our ability to express and imagine beyond conventional boundaries. This distinctive capability is especially pertinent to those in authority. When we, as people in power, release our expressions of song and praise, it communicates to others that they too can partake in such expressions.

Observing a figure of authority engage in gratitude to our God empowers others to be free, bold, and courageous in releasing their unique sound to the Lord. She expressed, "It's a distinctive resonance," and continued, "I, too, will offer praises to the Lord. I will extol the Lord, the

God of Israel, through my song." Within this perspective lies a profound space, embodying our responsibility in various pursuits. This encompasses Deborah's legacy, her battle—symbolizing the directive to guide people back to God, where we discover our essence, our voice, our distinct sound, and unleash our authentic roar. In essence, the notion of contrived adoration, orchestrated worship, and the replication of others, including the notion of idolized worship, disintegrates.

We have stepped into the authority of our identity in God, acknowledging and embracing our divine authority. Consequently, we have discovered ourselves. My aspiration is not to emulate another's sound; rather, I desire to resonate authentically, echoing the unique expression of God that glorifies Him, much like Keisha's distinctive roar, as it is my exclusive offering of worship. In this significant moment, the transformative power unfolded as individuals in positions of leadership and authority, exemplified by figures such as Deborah and Barak, released the divine essence. The subsequent response from the people was not a mere imitation of their leaders, but a genuine outpouring of personalized praises to their Creator. This was not an attempt to mimic the leadership; rather, it emanated from a desire to authentically express gratitude and worship.

Referencing the Scriptures, particularly in verse four, we observe a profound impact when the Lord's presence traversed from Seir and the land of Edom. The earth quaked, the heavens poured, clouds released water, and mountains trembled before the Lord, the God of Israel. In this divine expression, Deborah took the initiative to articulate the magnificence of God. Her words recounted the awe-inspiring moments when God's presence touched Edom, causing mountains to quake. Her narrative focused on God's majesty and power.

The consequence of Deborah's proclamation was a collective stirring among the people. They were reminded of the mightiness of their God, and this remembrance ignited a wave of worship. As you raise your voice in song and worship, it is crucial to recognize that your expressions have the potential to impact others profoundly. Just as Deborah spoke of the Lord's majesty, your worship can catalyze others to encounter God. Through your song, your bars, and your worship, others may find themselves overwhelmed by the sheer awesomeness of our God. Leading the charge in worship becomes an invitation for others to experience the mighty acts of God, creating a pathway for divine encounters.

Throughout Chapter 5 she began to speak so eloquently concerning the things that had transpired. In verse six she said, "In the days of Shamger son of Anath, in the days of Jael, the highways were abandoned; travelers took winding paths" (NIV). Villagers in Israel would not fight; they held back until Deborah arose, a mother in Israel. God chose new leaders when war came to the city. Why did God choose new leaders when war came into the city? Deborah rose. He chose new leaders, worship, and new Levites. He chose new psalmists. He chose new people to put in place because they saw the desolation.

Recognizing the challenges and concerns, you chose to emerge as a force for positive change. Your decision extended beyond assuming roles in authority, churches, business, and ministry; you embraced a pivotal position in worship. As you lifted your voice in song before the Lord, joy resonated, and the people, in turn, experienced gladness. This joyous transformation enabled them to connect with the God of their salvation, a divine presence beyond personal boundaries. Their newfound ability to sing praises before the Lord marked a shift in perspective, fostering a collective identification with the God who delivers.

In times of distress, when the city gates faced the specter of war, God intervened by appointing new leaders. Remarkably, amidst a congregation of 40,000 in Israel, not a single shield, spear, or weapon could be found. This absence of conventional defenses underscores the extraordinary nature of the divine intervention. The people's cry for help prompted God to raise leaders who, although lacking traditional armaments, embodied the essence of readiness and dedication.

In this critical moment, the focus shifted from the conventional instruments of war to the heart of Israel's princes and the dedication of willing volunteers among the people. Their commitment, unencumbered by visible weaponry, showcased a profound reliance on faith and divine guidance. This narrative underscores the transformative power of worship, the emergence of new leadership, and the significance of a community united in devotion and resolve. There was no weaponry found; only voices that echoed the space. If one delves into the scriptures and examines the sacred text, it becomes evident that many scenarios unfolded without the need for weapons; instead, the sound was resonant, the harmony of song, and the fervor of worship.

Numerous instances within the scriptures exemplify this phenomenon, with a personal favorite being the account of the walls of Jericho. In this narrative, the walls did not crumble under the assault of arrows, the storming of gates, or the ascent of climbers. It was the resounding release of the people's voices in that sacred atmosphere that caused the imposing walls to collapse flat to the ground. Understanding that there exists a profound resonance within, akin to a soulful pitch nestled in one's belly, empowers individuals to discern that by listening, one can invoke a transformative force against the opposition. Gratitude is expressed to the divine, acknowledging the alignment with purpose, destiny, and affirmation. When one opens their mouth in song, offering praise and worship to the God of salvation, it catalyzes the defeat of any opposing force hindering the divine purpose in one's life.

Referencing Judges 5:10, the imagery of those riding on white donkeys, symbolic of wealth and authority in certain cultures, and those walking along walls invites contemplation. The directive is to heed the voices of the singers at the watering places—locations of sustenance, nourishment, and restoration. These voices commemorate the triumphs of the Lord, celebrating victories not only for themselves but for the collective community in Israel. This call to sing praises extends to every circumstance, even when encountering individuals of influence and affluence. The metaphorical watering places, where nourishment and rejuvenation occur, become the backdrop for reciting the triumphs of the Lord. It serves as a reminder that in challenging moments, recalling past victories becomes the catalyst for a triumphant declaration.

During moments of adversity, when the memory falters and the path to victory seems unclear, the faithful are encouraged to recall God's past victories. These past triumphs serve as the spiritual ammunition needed to raise one's voice and release the soul in worship. In doing so, the barriers—reminiscent of the walls of Jericho—yield to the power of a sound grounded in the memory of previous seasons of divine intervention. The release of this sound becomes an act of faith, a declaration of trust in God's consistency, and a firm belief in the unfolding of victorious outcomes.

Judges 5:11-12 says, "…Then the people of the Lord went down to the city gates. Wake up, wake up, Deborah! Wake up, wake up, break out in song!" Break out in song and sing. Then verse 13-15 says, "The remnant of the nobles came down; the people of the Lord came down to me against the mighty." Some came from Ephraim whose roots were an Amalek; Benjamin was with the people who followed you. From Makir captains came down, from Zebulun those who bear a commander's staff. The princes of Issachar were with Deborah; yes. Issachar was with

Barak, sent under his command into the valley." We acknowledge that Issachar, as one of the twelve sons, possessed the ability to discern time.

As we engage in worship, song, and the release of sound, a divine dialogue unfolds. God imparts wisdom, insight, and knowledge, offering a profound understanding of the present moment. Could it be that as we persist in our devotion through worship, and song, seeking His presence, and attuning our ears to His voice, God will unveil the enigmatic truths and secrets concealed within the fabric of time? Might we, through this ongoing communion, gain the discernment needed to comprehend the complexities of our surroundings?

Now, turning our attention to verse 19, the scripture reveals, "Kings came, they fought, the kings of Canaan fought. At Taanach, by the waters of Megiddo, they took no plunder of silver. From the heavens, the stars fought, from their courses they fought against Sisera. The river of Kishon swept them away, the age-old river, the river Kishon. March on, my soul; be strong! Then thundered the horses' hooves-

galloping, galloping go his mighty steeds. Curse Merzo,' said the Angel of the Lord. 'Curse its people bitterly, because they did not come to help the Lord, to help the Lord against the mighty.'" Engaging in worship is not merely a routine or a passive response to God's blessings. God's interaction transcends mere blessings; it encompasses the impartation of insight, answers to lingering questions, and the bestowment of authority and power in unexplored realms, even those we haven't consciously sought.

The essence of worship lies in its ability to prompt God to reveal mysteries, to initiate a friendship, and to unveil hidden aspects of our existence. Worship, when approached with a pure and sincere heart, grants us access to the previously inaccessible. The act of worship becomes the key that unlocks doors to realms beyond our reach, transforming the once inaccessible into the readily available. It extends beyond the typical or the formerly untouchable, paving the way for revelations that would remain concealed without our worshipful connection. While others may shout or dance, true access to God requires a genuine, heartfelt worship that goes beyond mere performative acts.

Desiring the secrets of God while neglecting worship with a pure heart is a contradiction. We cannot expect to receive the profound and hidden aspects of divine understanding if we fail to approach God with clean hands and a pure heart. The responsibility of worship demands more than superficial actions; it necessitates a genuine connection with God that is rooted in sincerity. In our pursuit of God, it is imperative to acknowledge that worship is a responsibility. Longing for the things of God requires a commitment to worship characterized by clean hands and a pure heart. Unfortunately, the prevalence of offering up "strange fire" under the guise of worship has become a cultural norm within the Church.

To truly worship God is to rise above the cultural acceptance of substituting genuine praise with counterfeit offerings. It requires an understanding that clean hands and a pure heart are prerequisites for authentic worship. Without these, the worship becomes distorted, like offering up "strange fire" – a deviation from the genuine connection that God desires. Reflecting on the historical context of the 12 tribes of Israel, we see the consequences of deviating from authentic worship. The leaders' acknowledgment of the importance of clean hands and a pure heart influenced the people, leading them to willingly praise God. This understanding is a vital lesson for contemporary worshipers, emphasizing the need to forsake strange fire and embrace a worship that is sincere, pure, and transformative. In times of adversity, we invoke the Lord as our mighty instrument, dismantling the barriers that confront us. God directs us to discover our unique expression, promising to guide and instruct us in finding our distinctive voice. Embracing this personalized sound becomes a transformative force, empowering us to navigate the challenges we face.

Some among us find themselves singing the sacred melodies, echoing the sentiment expressed in scripture: "How can we sing the Lord's song in a foreign land?" This age-old inquiry resonates across time, questioning our ability to find harmony in discomfort, uncertainty, and adversity. Yet, the unwavering truth is that the song of the Lord remains constant.

When we courageously lift our voices in worship, even amid unfamiliarity and unwanted circumstances, a remarkable shift occurs. Our focus is redirected from the strange and desolate surroundings, shifting towards God and His triumphant nature. In the face of discomfort and uncertainty, our worship serves as a powerful connector to the divine, turning our attention away from the unfamiliar and deadly terrain. The timeless truth, rooted in the Bible, asserts that God resides in the praises of His people. Through our worship, we transcend the strangeness, desolation, and peril of our surroundings, creating a sacred space where God's presence is keenly felt. The once unfamiliar and perilous landscape is transformed into a sanctuary of divine connection and empowerment.

Expressing gratitude and acknowledging God's victories, we declare that the strange land is no longer unfamiliar, and the deadly place is now infused with divine grace. The transformative power of worship allows us to navigate through the valleys, echoing the reassurance found in Psalm 23:4: "Yea, though I walk through the valley of the shadow of death, I will fear no evil, for thou art with me; thy rod and thy staff, they comfort me."

Amid this valley, fear finds no foothold, for Your presence accompanies me. Our songs, our praises, and our worship transform these seemingly separated and chaotic spaces into sanctuaries, as I have chosen to make the Lord my dwelling place. Even though physically situated in the same circumstances, my refuge is found in God, regardless of what challenges I face. I sing before the Lord, offering my worship and praise, creating melodies that resonate with His desires. I allow the Holy Spirit to give birth to the divine within me, echoing the sentiment of Deborah's song in Chapter 5. Her anthem wasn't crafted by a Levite or commissioned by a musician; it emerged from the depths of her being, a song born out of uncertainty, pain, and trial. She recognized the hand of her God in her victories, urging others to remember and sing of the Lord's triumphs.

So, I echo the call to change the channel of my song, to sing a new melody that acknowledges the victories, the deliverance, and the grace bestowed upon me. I am reminded to sing over my loved ones, to vocalize the song of God's favor over my family and those who are dear to me. It is this unique sound, emanating from the depth of my being, that causes the enemy to scatter in disarray. In unfamiliar places, I am encouraged to sing, for in the melody of the Lord's song, victory unfolds, adversity trembles, and the enemy retreats. This is a reminder to rise and sing, not just for myself but for generations to come. I am prompted to sing over my children, grandchildren, nieces, nephews, and every significant relationship in my life. It is through this intentional act of singing that the atmosphere shifts and the enemy is forced to flee in multiple directions. The charge is clear: sing in the face of uncertainty, sing over challenges, and sing despite unfavorable news.

In the act of singing, I invite the divine into my circumstances. So, I choose to sing over my husband, my father, my mother, and even over those who may be counted as adversaries. It's time to replace complaints and worries with melodies of gratitude and trust. As I lift my voice, I usher in the presence of God, and victory becomes the anthem that resonates in every corner of my life. It's your sound that will set them free. Take note of how scripture emphasizes singing and worship. In Exodus 15, it was after the song was released that they were delivered. It's not until we sing the song of the Lord that we are truly set free. It's the soundtrack of your life, the melody of your soul, and the rhythm of your heart.

In conclusion, Deborah's story reminds us of the profound impact of worship and the transformative power of song. As poets, we wield a unique authority to craft words that resonate with divine truth and invoke God's presence. Just as Deborah's song inspired victory among the Israelites, our worship has the potential to usher in divine breakthroughs in our lives and the lives of those around us. Let us embrace our authority as worshipers and leaders, releasing our unique sound to the Lord. As we sing praises amid adversity, let us remember that our worship is a powerful weapon against the enemy. May our songs of gratitude and praise echo throughout the ages, ushering in God's kingdom here on earth. And as we raise our voices in worship, may we experience the fullness of God's presence and the abundant life He has promised us. Amen.

Closing Prayer

Father, bless us thank you so much for being God thank you for strengthening us thank you God for giving us the courage reminding us God remind us that our soul means something and that we don't have to pretend to fabricate and manufacture anything because you've given us what we need what you want to hear so father gives us the courage to come to you and ask you what you want excuse me from us father I thank you for this time thank you for bless us now for that bind all attacks our mental and emotional state. God even the things that come into our spirit. God, I find all acts of retaliation against this word because Father I believe that someone's chains will be annihilated, not broken but destroyed, and that the voice of the liar and the deceiver can no longer pull on the emotions of their people. Father, I pray that everyone who encounters this word of God is changed and renewed immediately because of you and would you have spoken. Father, I thank you that you have caused us to sing. In Jesus name, Amen.

Chapter 11

Deborah the Fearless

Have you been praising, child? Have you ever risen and lifted your voice in song? We delved into the poet singing in the last chapter, and this chapter, we're diving into the fearless. We've been in Judges 4 for the past few sessions, and that's where we find ourselves. But let me tell you, I won't be sticking to just one verse, I'll be leaping through the scripture because we've truly delved into it. What I really want us to hone in on is being unshakable in our pursuit of God—unwavering and unafraid in all things concerning the Almighty.

Fearlessness, my sister, is more than just the absence of fear. It's about bravely standing in the face of danger, possessing a spirit that enables you to confront challenges without showing a hint of fear. It's about being in situations that should naturally evoke fear, yet having the audacity, the self-control, and the understanding of self to exude fearlessness.

Let's dive into the story of our sister Deborah, a powerful woman, a prophet, and a judge. In those days, women were not esteemed as they are today. The value placed on women, their power, and influence were not as prevalent back then. It wasn't common for women to hold positions of authority or step into roles of leadership, especially during tumultuous times. Yet here we witness the extraordinary – a woman of war, a woman of strategy, a woman chosen by the Lord. Despite societal norms and expectations, Deborah emerged as a beacon of strength and wisdom. She faced challenges that would typically be handled by men, yet she stood firm, unyielding in her fearlessness.

Beloved, let this be a testament to the transformative power of God. He elevates and empowers, regardless of societal limitations. Deborah's story teaches us that, even in times when society might undervalue us, God sees our worth and calls us to positions of influence. So, let us embrace the spirit of fearlessness, knowing that with God, we can navigate any situation with grace, strength, and unwavering confidence.

Sister Deborah was summoned once more, and let me tell you, Israel had found themselves deep in yet another mess of their own making. God had to swoop in and rescue them, but this time, the Most High took a different route. The Almighty chose a woman, yes, He chose her and placed her in a position of influence, power, and authority. Let me emphasize, she walked in those realms fearlessly because she knew who she was, fully aware and understanding.

Now, don't get it twisted; Deborah's mission wasn't a walk in the park. Picture this: she's a general leading the troops into battle. War, my sisters and brothers, means potential casualties, the risk of being beaten down, thrown away – a whole heap of scenarios that usually belong to the menfolk in war. Now, insert a woman into the mix. We all know too well that women can become casualties of war in ways I won't delve into right now. Yet, with all this knowledge, she stepped into these situations, fully aware of the dangers that could come her way.

Let me tell you something about Deborah. She walked in there with her head held high because she knew who she was in the eyes of God. Danger was all around her, yes, but she walked in fearlessly. She walked in with courage. She walked in with control, exuding a spirit that enabled her to face danger head-on without buckling, running, or fleeing. Her mission was perilous, no doubt, but the potential danger didn't dictate her actions. It didn't tell her how to behave, respond, or carry out the mission God called her to. Why? Because she fully comprehended who it was that sent her. She stood firm, unwavering, and unyielding in the face of danger, all because of her understanding of the God who commissioned her.

You must walk in the boldness of the Lord, especially in what He's called you to do. There comes a divine moment when God expects us to grasp, rely on, welcome, and confront without flinching every potential challenge. God wants us to confront it full-on, armed with the awareness that He stands by our side. You see, fear creeps in when we attempt to tackle it apart from God. When we charge ahead, relying on our own strength, that's what makes us pull back when faced with danger, discomfort, criticism, and opposition. Those are the triggers for retreat, causing us to run and shrink away because we lack a complete understanding of the One who called and chose us. We stumble when we enter the battle in our own might, treating God as an option instead of recognizing Him as the priority, the necessity, the requirement.

Deborah stepped into this situation covered, and it wasn't the armies or her position as a prophet or judge that shielded her. No, what protected Deborah in that dangerous moment was her obedience to God. Many of us find ourselves feeling exposed and vulnerable because we hesitate to obey the Lord, neglecting his statutes and lacking reverence for him. When we compromise and disregard what God deems holy, we end up in compromising situations. It was Deborah's obedience that led her into potential danger but kept her protected. It was her reverence for God and adherence to His commands that shielded her in the midst of a war, not just any war, but a war where a woman stood against the world. Her obedience to God was her protection.

Here's the deal; it doesn't mean the enemy couldn't see her or access her in that situation. What it means is that because she made the Lord her dwelling place and hiding place, she found protection. Her obedience allowed her to operate fearlessly, not without danger, but the danger didn't matter because she walked in with God, armed with his instructions, under his rule.

For us, there are certain things, especially those related to the Lord, where our obedience will keep us covered and shielded. This isn't limited to ministry; it extends to various calls God has placed on our lives—business, entrepreneurship, leadership, humility, forgiveness, and more. The call to God brings automatic opposition because the enemy doesn't want us to fully understand who we are. It's time to break free from limiting ourselves to societal expectations and come into a fearless pursuit of God.

When you've been called by God, opposition is a given because the devil doesn't want you to realize your authority and influence, which goes beyond preaching or being connected to someone in authority. The call of God on your life brings you into power, influence, and authority. Fearlessness means pursuing God without concern for others' opinions or validation because you've heard God's voice for yourself. Stop limiting yourself out of fear. The story of Deborah, a woman rising in a time when societal norms confined women to homemaking, showcases God's choice of someone willing to obey and trust Him.

When you walk in fearlessness, you walk with the assurance that you are not alone, that God is with you. Man's opinion and validation become irrelevant because you've heard the voice of God. The reason we struggle with fearlessness is that we often try to be our own coverings, attempting to play God. But how's that working out for you? How has covering yourself worked so far?

We often confine God within the boundaries of our own experiences. But let me tell you, he's the one who can rewrite those very experiences. Do you grasp the concept that the God Deborah walked with is the creator and author of time? Deborah understood this truth, yet we keep missing it by limiting God to our understanding. The Bible wisely instructs, "Lean not to your own understanding but in all your ways acknowledge him" (Proverbs 3:5-6). Deborah's protection came from acknowledging him, and even in the midst of war, He directed her path because she acknowledged him.

I consistently share with people that I am completely and utterly dependent on Him. Without Him, I can do nothing. I may try to operate in my giftedness, but it pales in comparison to His glory and His presence with me. My gift is insignificant compared to His glory. Without Him, nothing matters. He is an absolute necessity for me. To walk fearlessly in the calling He has placed on my life, I must seek Him for guidance on how it should be done.

In the book of Judges, when the people cried out, Deborah rose, and the Lord began to speak to her, strategizing with her, giving her divine insight. Deborah, in turn, passed on the strategy to the general, and they executed perfectly. To ensure that only God received the glory, the prophet told the general, "Listen, God will give us the victory, but it won't happen the way you expect. A woman named Jael will bring down the enemy." God orchestrated the victory using the uncertain and the uncommon in that hour. Their obedience made them fearless, not relying on their own strength or authority.

What if we chose to lay down our own authority and let the Lord cover us? We would operate under the authority of God as His sons and daughters. Many claim to be sons, but they lack submission and obedience. Gifts may come without repentance, but it's the anointing that breaks the yoke. We have an abundance of gifts, but not enough true sons. Deborah was a daughter, accessing authority through submission. Because she was a submitted son and daughter, she tapped into real power.

We often function in disobedience, behaving like bastards rather than accessing the true power of God. Consequently, we walk into situations full of fear and uncertainty. The question is, who's your Daddy? Are you a son or a bastard? I know someone's got my back, and I am not afraid. Do you truly understand who is protecting and covering you? Sons and daughters operate under the authority of the Father with full instruction, knowledge, and understanding. They can deliver messages and strategies fearlessly because they have a direct connection to the Father. On the other hand, those who are not sons or daughters are inconsistent and double-minded because their ears are not attuned to the voice of the Father. Consequently, they appear fearless until faced with danger, revealing their true fears because they are not anchored in the Father's voice.

You can't step into the situation without a hint of fear. When danger shows up, you run, retreat, and rebel out of fear. The truth is, I can't hear clearly because there are too many other voices clamoring for my attention. Either I can hear, but I choose not to listen because I'm afraid of what He might say. I cloak myself in church accolades, busywork, and an array of hats. I conceal myself beneath these gabardine suits, lap rags, and collars adorned with significant crosses and Bibles. I bury myself in various committees, titles, and positions—all because I'm avoiding hearing. If only you'd listen to His voice and his word, you'd discover that all these things we hide behind are unnecessary. Once you realize you don't need them, you won't want them. To be fearless means emerging from hiding. Stop hiding from God, from yourself, and from your critics. It's time to step out of hiding.

Now, let's delve into the Scriptures. I'm reminded of the passage when Elijah became scared and sought refuge in a cave. In 1 Kings 19:10, it says, "There he went into a cave and spent the night, and the word of the Lord came to him. 'What are you doing here, Elijah?'" Elijah responded, "I have been very zealous for the Lord God Almighty. The Israelites have rejected your covenant, torn down your altars, and put your prophets to death with the sword. I'm the only one left, and now they're trying to kill me too." Elijah sought refuge in a cave out of fear because God had been rejected, the covenant was broken, altars were destroyed, and prophets were killed. Elijah decided to hide rather than face the threat. Then the Lord said, "Go out and stand on the mountain, for the Lord is about to pass by.

In this passage, we see Elijah, a mighty prophet of God, succumbing to fear and seeking refuge in a cave. He felt isolated and alone, believing that he was the only faithful one left and that his life was in danger. But God's response to Elijah's fear was not one of condemnation but of reassurance and guidance. He called Elijah out of the cave to stand on the mountain, signaling that He was about to reveal Himself powerfully.

Like Elijah, we often find ourselves in situations where fear grips us and causes us to hide away, avoiding the challenges and threats we face. But God doesn't want us to cower in fear; He wants us to stand boldly and trust in Him. He calls us out of our hiding places, promising to reveal Himself and provide the strength and guidance we need to face whatever comes our way.

When we walk in fearlessness, we walk in the confidence of knowing that God is with us, guiding us every step of the way. We don't need to rely on our strength or understanding because we have the assurance that God is in control. So let us heed God's call to step out of hiding, stand boldly on the mountain, and trust in His power to overcome every obstacle and challenge we face.

Closing Prayer

Father, I pray God that you approved every root and every suggestion of fear in our lives. God calls us to come and sit under the palm tree where we can hear your voice for strategy and instruction, and then execute fearlessly concerning which you have spoken to us. Father, I pray God that as we walk in obedience, our obedience covers us just like it covered Deborah. God that because of our obedience, lives or changed, our lives are changed, and we walk into destiny moments, connections and resources that produce miracles in the lives of your people. Father, I thank you God that you've chosen us as sons in this hour. Father, we humbly submit, commit, and repent for not trusting your voice concerning us. We submit now to your voice, to your will, and to your desire for us because it's better anyway. We don't know what we're doing. We need you. So, we humbly accept and embrace you, your desires, your voice, your wants, and your love for us. We no longer make excuses and go hide because we're scared. You're a good and an amazing Father. We love you. Thank you for choosing us Jesus name, Amen.

Chapter 12

Deborah the Courageous

As we draw near to the conclusion of our journey, reflecting on the profound influence of our beloved Prophetess Deborah's life, we eagerly anticipate hearing the wisdom the Lord has to impart. I'll do my best to tie it all together, allowing God to lead the way. Throughout our exploration, we've delved into various aspects of Prophetess Deborah's character through tears, prayers, and heartfelt discussions. Our final focus rests on the courage that accompanies the journey of being courageous.

Courage demands a steadfast mindset, an awareness of one's capabilities, and a deep understanding of what it means to proceed with courage. Joshua 1:9 from the Amplified Bible underscores this, "Have I not commanded you? Be strong and courageous! Do not be terrified or dismayed, for the Lord your God is with you wherever you go." God reminds us that as we pursue our divine callings, strength is essential. Courage entails confronting dangers and difficulties with unwavering resolve. God's question resonates: "Didn't I command you to be strong?" This implies that strength is a prerequisite for the journey God has called us to, and courage means facing challenges firmly without intimidation, dismay, or fear because God is with us.

Deborah's story epitomizes courage in the face of adversity. Her understanding that victory came from the One who chose her empowered her to stand firm and deliver God's word. Despite challenges and lack of universal acceptance, Deborah chose courage, strength, and an unwavering commitment to her purpose. She refused to be intimidated or terrified, knowing that the Lord God would be with her wherever she went.

As we conclude this journey, I urge you to choose courage in pursuing your destiny and purpose. Embrace your incredible and unique self without intimidation or persuasion by circumstances. Break free from the conditioning of your past and muster the courage to boldly align with God's plan for your life. Roar, woman! Release your unique sound with courage and embrace your purpose, knowing that not everyone may agree or embrace it. Courage eliminates excuses and demands responsibility and accountability. Acknowledge the potential dangers and difficulties, but proceed with the understanding that God is with you. You can walk into the destiny God has called you to. Be your most authentic self, take comfort, and find courage in the assurance that God is with you.

Cease being terrified of potential outcomes and relinquish feeling intimidated by external expectations. You have a unique call and anointing. You are predestined, just like Deborah, uniquely fashioned for the purpose God has called you to. Embrace your identity without fear, knowing that being yourself can break familial bonds. God is not merely asking; He's commanding you. Be courageous, be affirmed, be tested, be anointed, be healed, and be unapologetically true to yourself.

You are righteous, set apart, and deemed worthy by the Almighty. Let God revel in the magnificence of your life. Refrain from fleeing from fear and instead, embrace your worthiness. You are a divine melody, a sacred verse, a living testament—God yearns for your existence. No more justifications; embody prayer, intercession, evangelism, teaching, or whatever role God calls you to fulfill. Be bold, for God has entrusted you. In whatever 'be' He beckons you to, embrace it wholeheartedly and with unwavering courage.

Become the very thing you've been avoiding. Confront and embody what you've been evading. Be the transformation you aspire to witness. If you sought a guide, become one. If you longed for a nurturing presence, step into that maternal role. Whatever your 'be' may be, fully embody it. Embrace courage in your essence; be authentically you. Cease the unnecessary apologies and simply be, for God relies on you to manifest His divine plan.

Do not let that devil scare you for one more day, beloved. Do not let the enemy, with all his tricks and traps, make you feel small for one more day. The Lord, our God, has unequivocally commanded you to be bold and brave. He's telling you, "Do not you dare let fear take hold of you. I need you to occupy and claim your space, child." Pray those big prayers, prayers that make you shiver a bit. It's time to speak up and ask for what God's been waiting for us to request. We've been holding back, too scared to utter it, too afraid to declare it. It's time for courage, y'all.

We've been hesitating to step into certain realms, to commit to God in certain places, all because we're scared of what the enemy might throw at us. But I'm here to tell you, there's a boldness about to fall on the people of God. When that enemy tries to rear his ugly head, we won't cower. No, we'll stand tall and courageous. We won't let the enemy's suggestions rattle us because we've been trained to worry about warfare when God's shouting, "Be strong and courageous!" Do not let fear and intimidation hold you back because God is right there with you, wherever your journey takes you.

We've been hesitant, hesitant to move where God has called us because of the fear of attack. Well, listen closely, beloved. God is saying, "Be bold. Be courageous. Be strong. Do not let intimidation paralyze you because I'm right there with you, no matter where you go." You need to hear that, absorb it, and let it fuel your courage. Isaiah 59:19 reminds us that when the enemy comes in like a flood, it's not us, it's God who raises a standard against him. Let that truth soak into your spirit. God's got your back, and it's time to stand tall in the face of fear.

The reason why our sister Deborah displayed such boldness is because she grasped the truth that wherever she stepped, God was right there by her side. She also comprehended the power of worship, as we saw in Judges 5 where she poured out her heart in worship. Deborah recognized the transformative impact of habitual worship. When we engage in consistent worship, it compels God to linger, to dwell, and to abide in our midst.

The Scriptures affirm that He resides in the praises of His people—that's His dwelling place. So, when we make habitual worship a part of our lives, we internalize the essence of being strong and courageous because we've already immersed ourselves in worship. We've already spent precious moments in His presence. Understanding the profound exchange in worship eliminates any grounds for fear, intimidation, or dismay, for I've already immersed myself in worship with Him.

As I engage in the rhythm of worship and praise, I usher God into my space. If the adversary decides to approach, he's not just confronting me; he's facing God. My sister reminded me, and I'm grateful to God for it. The enemy wages war against us, but he can't contend with God. So, as the people of God, we must ensure that we incorporate God into every aspect. That's how we elevate the standard—bringing Him into the equation through worship, praise, and encounters.

We must make practicing His presence a habit. Why should I feel intimidated or fearful when I walk in His presence? It's akin to facing a bully on the street, turning to the side, and saying, "You want to deal with this? Look who's right here." We often leave God out of the equation, failing to bring Him in, leading to intimidation and fear persisting.

Remember, we can't be courageous without Him. We can't fight without Him. We must include Him, engage Him, and make Him a part of our lives. Just like the courageous woman who included God and stood fearlessly in dangerous situations, we too can stand tall when we include Him. It's not a false sense of courage; it's a deep understanding of who God is and, consequently, who we are in Him.

When we make His presence our habitation, distractions lose their power. What many experiences are not attacks but distractions—taps on the window trying to lure us out of the safety of God's presence. Don't be swayed; stay covered. Just as a child goes to their daddy when bothered, go to God, and let Him handle the distractions. Don't let the enemy distract you from being courageous and strong in God. So, be courageous, be bold, be unapologetically courageous. God has commanded it because He is with you wherever you go.

Closing prayer

Father, I thank you. It is only because of your grace and your love for us that you have brought us through this journey. you have brought this assignment to completion. Father, I pray in Jesus' name that every woman that comes across these teachings that every life will be changed because you have changed mine. Father, I thank you for prophet Deborah and her example, her spirit, her mantle, and the anointing of Deborah. Father, I pray as we conclude this study that we see ourselves and our sister and God and that you make it more evident than ever before. You've called us to trailblaze, to lead, to agitate, to prophesy, to heal, to be courageous, and to be fearless. God, you have called us to one or all the twelve things covered in this book so that you can make us a weapon against the enemy. Father, I pray that we take the courage with which you have spoken. Take courage in your voice. Take courage in your presence knowing that you have equipped us to do the very thing that we are afraid of. We don't need to be concerned about the tapping at the window because you're in the house. So, Father, we take on your authority and your permission to be courageous, not intimidated, and to be strong because you are with us wherever we go. Father, thank you for choosing us for this time. We love you. In Jesus name, Amen.

Chapter 13

Weapons of Mass

Destruction

In the book of Joshua, chapter 6, verse 20, the King James Version states, "So the people shouted when the priests blew the trumpets: and it came to pass, when the people heard the sound of the trumpet, and the people shouted with a great shout, that the wall fell down flat, so that the people went up into the city, every man straight before him, and they took the city. 21 And they destroyed all that was in the city." The Amplified Version reads, "So the people shouted [the battle cry] and the priests blew the trumpets. When the people heard the trumpet, they raised a great shout and the wall [of Jericho] fell, so that the sons of Israel went up into the city, every man straight ahead, [climbing over the rubble] and they overthrew the city. 21 Then they destroyed everything that was in the city."

We need to wake up because God has called us to interrupt cycles—we are weapons of mass destruction. Our roar, our sound, are our weapons of mass destruction. That's why the devil doesn't want you to ever find out who you are. He never wants us to wake up because he knows if we ever find out who we are and get up, we're going to interrupt cycles in our generations.

A weapon of mass destruction is defined as a chemical, biological, or radioactive weapon capable of causing widespread death and destruction (Dictionary.com). So here we are in Joshua, the children of Israel are now looking at what is called Jericho. If you do a little biblical research, you'll see that Jericho is surrounded by a wall—it's a fortified city, meaning no one can get in and no one can get out. They roll up to a place where there is no easy entry. But if you go back to the beginning of the chapter, the Lord spoke to Joshua and said, "Look, I've given you this city. You can't get in and nobody can get out."

What do you mean, you've given me the city? Nobody can get in there, and the folks in there can't get out. So, the Lord instructed Joshua what to do with the priests and the people, which brings me to my first point: You have to utilize your weapon. The first thing you've got to be is obedient. Whatever the Lord is telling you to do, woman or gentleman, the first thing you have to do is obey. What does that look like? Go start that book, start the church, go back to school, move to another state—just obey the instruction. That's number one.

The next point is this: When the people were given the instruction from their leader, the next thing they did was act in faith. The Bible says that faith pleases God. Sometimes we obey, but we don't believe. That's why there is no manifestation. For the walls to fall flat in your life, you've got to believe that the instruction you're given is going to bear fruit. They had to believe that the sound they released was going to produce what they were expecting.

So here they are, they walk up to this fortified city and the instruction was to walk around it. No one can get in and no one can get out. Not only did they have to walk, but they had to walk around it seven times. Jericho is not the largest city in the Bible, but nonetheless, it is a city. They had to walk around it for seven days, and you see why they needed faith and why they needed to obey. What would have happened if they had walked around, it seven times in one day? The walls wouldn't have fallen because that wasn't the instruction. Obedience is exact and immediate.

If God tells you to go left two steps, don't go left three steps and expect him to move. The instruction was to walk around the fortified city. At some point, they might have thought this wasn't going to work. They probably doubted and thought Joshua was crazy, the priests were crazy, God was crazy. Everyone was crazy, talking about walking around a city in the desert—it's hot! I would have been in the group complaining, "Y'all, it's hot. Let's set up a tent and try again tomorrow."

I'm sure there were moments of emotional fatigue, but they continued walking. I'm driving this point because all of us have a Jericho we are walking around. Everybody has a Jericho. You know, walking around this addiction, walking around this child, walking around this crazy man or woman. I'm tired of walking around this poverty in my bloodline, tired of walking around wanting a house and not getting one, tired of walking around this dead-end job, tired of walking around trying to get this degree, tired of walking around being sick and attacked by disease. I'm tired of walking around this church with folks that don't want to serve and believe You, but I'm walking around it because You said so. Walking around because You told me to walk around these disobedient children, these rebellious situations.

The Lord instructed them to walk around seven times, and on the seventh day, they were to walk around the city seven times and then shout. On that day, the shout and the trumpet were the beginning to an end. The walls fell because they obeyed the instruction completely and precisely. Obedience is exact and immediate.

God has called us to use our voices as weapons. The Bible says that the weapons of our warfare are not carnal but mighty through God to the pulling down of strongholds (2 Corinthians 10:4). Our worship, our praise, our prayers—they are powerful weapons. There is a sound within us that disrupts the enemy's plans. When the Israelites shouted, the walls of Jericho fell. Our sound has that same power to break strongholds and destroy barriers in our lives and the lives of others.

In Jeremiah 9:17, it talks about calling for the wailing women, those who were skilled in lamentation, to raise a cry because their sound had the power to move heaven. Women have a unique ability to release a sound that captures God's attention. A mother's ability to recognize her child's cry among many others is a testament to this. We have to release our sound. Don't let the enemy silence you. Your sound is unique and necessary. The world needs what is inside you. God has given you a mandate.

Don't delay. If He told you to start a prayer group, do it. The earth needs what is in you. We are weapons of mass destruction against the enemy's plans. Release your sound. God wants our roar, our sound, our voice. He called us, not us pretending to be something or somebody else. Be who you are. When God made you, He said it was very good (Genesis 1:31). You are enough. You are perfect just as you are. Don't waste time trying to conform to someone else's idea of who you should be. Be obedient to God's call and have faith in what He has said about you.

We need to come up higher and fight in heavenly places. This surpasses carnal desires—it's about accessing spiritual gifts and weaponry. Your sound is important. Your sound is needed. Don't ever let the enemy scare you into silence. Release what God has put in you. The world is calling out for it. Don't delay.

Pursue your dreams, answer your calling, and fulfill your purpose. You are an essential part of what God wants to do on Earth. Be the trailblazer, the truth-teller, the warrior, the ruler. Be fearless, be free. In Jesus' name, Amen. Thank you for joining me on this journey. I pray you are strengthened. Be courageous; you are built for this.
I love you.

Made in the USA
Columbia, SC
01 July 2024

37851624R00075